EASTER HANDBOOK

by Ramona Warren
Beth Holzbauer
Jane Belk Moncure
Annetta Dellinger
Dotti Hannum
Mae Aldous Kidman
and others

illustrated by Mina Gow McLean

THE CHILD'S WORLD

ELGIN, ILLINOIS 60120

EDITORS: Evelyn Solomon, Diane Dow Suire

Distributed by Childrens Press, 1224 West Van Buren Street Chicago, Illinois 60607

Library of Congress Cataloging in Publication Data

Warren, Ramona.
  Easter handbook.

  1. Easter decorations.   2. Handicraft.   3. Easter.
I. McLean, Mina Gow.   II. Title.
TT900.E2W37   1985   790.1'922   85-24322
ISBN 0-89565-306-0

1 2 3 4 5 6 7 8 9 10 R 92 91 90 89 88 87 86

EASTER HANDBOOK

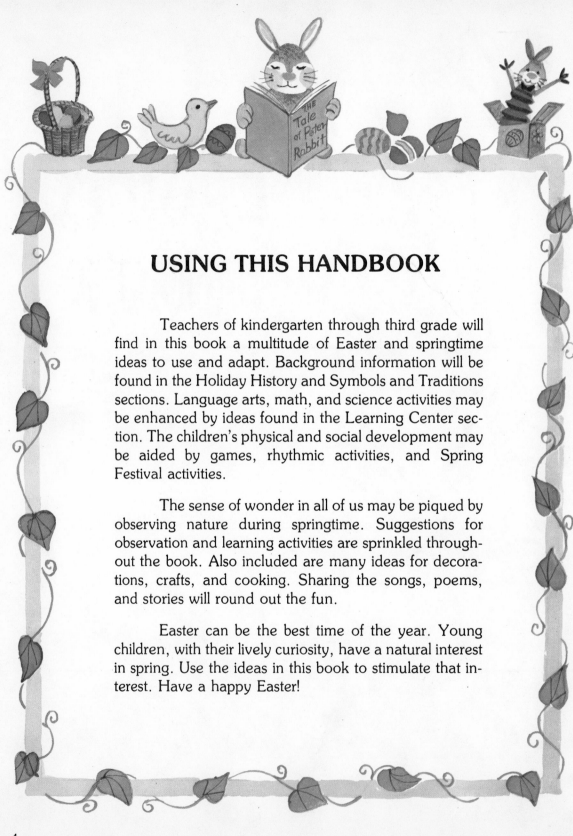

USING THIS HANDBOOK

Teachers of kindergarten through third grade will find in this book a multitude of Easter and springtime ideas to use and adapt. Background information will be found in the Holiday History and Symbols and Traditions sections. Language arts, math, and science activities may be enhanced by ideas found in the Learning Center section. The children's physical and social development may be aided by games, rhythmic activities, and Spring Festival activities.

The sense of wonder in all of us may be piqued by observing nature during springtime. Suggestions for observation and learning activities are sprinkled throughout the book. Also included are many ideas for decorations, crafts, and cooking. Sharing the songs, poems, and stories will round out the fun.

Easter can be the best time of the year. Young children, with their lively curiosity, have a natural interest in spring. Use the ideas in this book to stimulate that interest. Have a happy Easter!

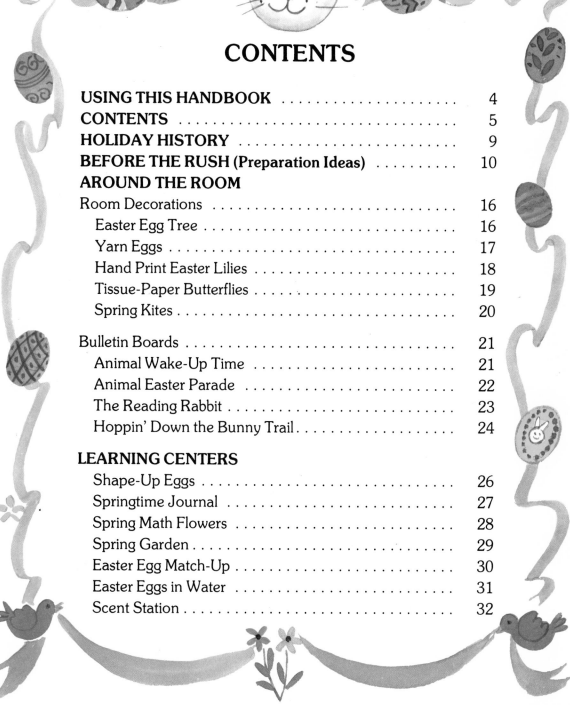

CONTENTS

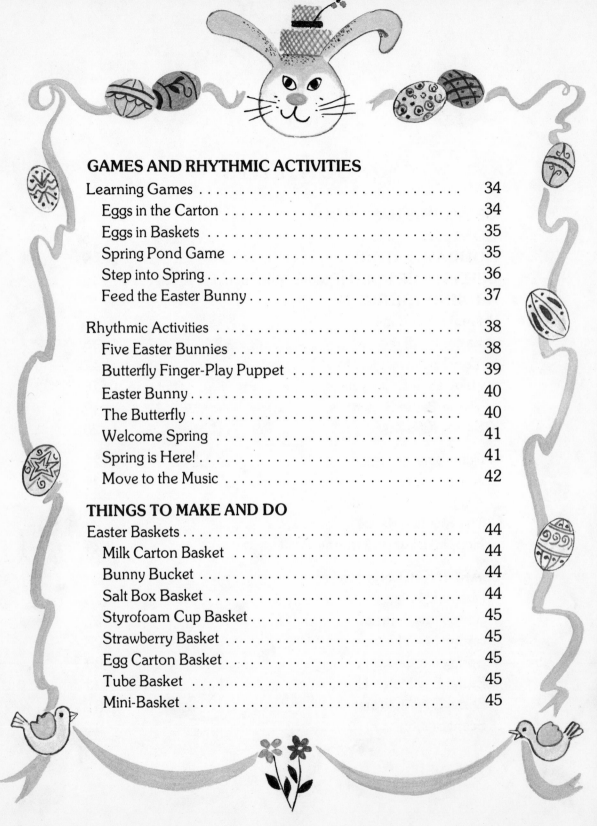

GAMES AND RHYTHMIC ACTIVITIES

THINGS TO MAKE AND DO

HOLIDAY HISTORY

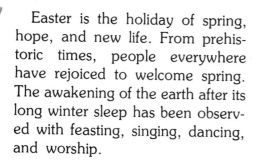

Easter is the holiday of spring, hope, and new life. From prehistoric times, people everywhere have rejoiced to welcome spring. The awakening of the earth after its long winter sleep has been observed with feasting, singing, dancing, and worship.

In America and most European countries, Easter is traditionally a Christian holiday. On this day, Christians celebrate the resurrection of Jesus Christ from the dead, as it is told in the Bible. This holy day celebrates the triumph of life over death.

Historically, the resurrection of Christ occurred at the time of the Jewish feast of Passover (called "Pesach" in Hebrew). In the early years of Christianity, Jewish Christians observed the resurrection and Passover together on the 14th day of Nisan, the Jewish month roughly corresponding to April. However, Gentile Christians celebrated the resurrection every Sunday with a special emphasis on the Sunday closest to Nisan 14. To settle this difference, at the Nicene Council in 325 A.D., churchmen fixed the date of Easter on the first Sunday following the Paschal full moon. That is the first full moon after the vernal equinox, March 21. This system is still followed today. Therefore, Easter Sunday moves between March 22 and April 25.

The term "Easter" was first used when Christianity was introduced to the Saxons. Prior to this time the Saxons had held an annual feast in honor of the ancient Teutonic goddess of spring, Eostre. The name was transferred to the Christian observance of Christ's resurrection.

People of many lands and languages have given various names to the celebration of spring. Through the years a great assortment of customs and traditions have developed. As people have emigrated, their customs have blended with native observances, till now the arrival of spring is acknowledged in a multitude of ways. But wherever and however Easter is kept, it is universally a joyous, happy day.

BEFORE THE RUSH

(Preparation Ideas)

To avoid the last minute rush, plan well ahead for celebrating the Easter season. Here are some suggestions for possible activities.

BOOK NOOK

Read a story about Easter or springtime. Below is a list of possibilities. Others may be found in the children's department of your local library.

- *The Bunny Who Knew All About Plants*
- *Bunches and Bunches of Bunnies*
- *The Tale of Peter Rabbit*
- *First Day of Spring*
- *Home for a Bunny*
- *The Bunny Book*
- *What's Inside: The Story of an Egg That Hatched*
- *Horton Hatches the Egg*
- *Runaway Bunny*
- *Chicken Little, Count-to-Ten*

PETS AT SCHOOL

Keep a pet or more in the classroom. If mates are kept, be prepared for babies from time to time. Fish in a tank with a filter are some of the easiest pets to keep.

Hamsters are clean and require only a little food and water and a change of nesting material once or twice a week. Gerbils are similar to hamsters and are more active during the daytime. Rabbits are wonderful classroom pets, but they require a lot of work unless you have a very good, easy-to-clean cage arrangement.

Turtles are interesting, especially if they can be housed in a fish tank with about six inches of water, so that they can dive and swim.

A toad or a salamander would feel at home in a woodland terrarium. It would need only some garden dirt, grass, a few stones, and a water dish. A salamander likes moist moss and pieces of decaying wood.

PLANTS AT SCHOOL

Many bulbs, root plants, seeds, and plant cuttings are easy to grow. Forsythia, pussy willow, and some of the fruit trees may be forced to bloom early by cutting their branches and putting them in water. Record the growth of the plants by drawing pictures on a large calendar or by making charts or graphs.

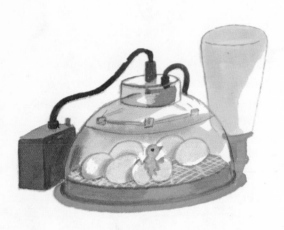

HATCHING EGGS

Hens' eggs take twenty-one days to hatch. They may share a nest or incubator with ducks' eggs, which take twenty-eight days. Here are a variety of ways that this wonder-filled project may be accomplished. Choose the way that's best for you.

1. Buy a hen and a clutch of eggs and watch her hatch them. Hen food, baby chick food and a watering container are needed besides a hen house of some sort.

2. Borrow an incubator and buy fertile eggs from a hatchery. Follow the instructions included.

3. Buy or borrow a small, two-egg incubator and buy two eggs that only have a few days left to mature so you will not have to wait so long for baby chicks to hatch.

4. Make an incubator and buy fertile eggs. A nearby 4-H office, poultry farmer, hatchery, or the agricultural department of a university can direct you. How-to information may also be obtained from books in your public library.

DRAMATIC PRESENTATION

The Tale of Peter Rabbit, by Beatrix Potter, is an old favorite. Prepare a tape recording of this story with your class, using sound effects. Let the children illustrate the story on drawing paper or pantomime the action. Present the production to another class.

SUPPLY CLOSET

by Beth Holzbauer

Send a letter home to your students' parents requesting scraps of odds and ends that will make the children's craft time more fun and interesting.

Organize the supplies into the following three categories: the Paper Patch (all paper materials), the Scrap Trap (miscellaneous trims, lace, feathers, etc.), and the Flower Garden (dried, plastic, or silk flowers).

Display the supplies in an attractive way, if possible. For instance, the Scrap Trap could be put in a large fish bowl or glass jar where it would arouse interest and choices could be easily seen. Cut any large items (a bouquet of flowers, yards of lace, wallpaper, etc.) into smaller pieces that can be used by individuals.

Paper Patch

Scrap Trap

Flower Garden

FIELD TRIPS

Plan a field trip to observe new life. See the baby animals at a zoo or petting farm. Arrange a tour to a poultry farm or hatchery to view the hatching process. A walk around the community or in a park provides an opportunity to see the awakening of plants that are dormant in the winter. A field trip may be easily combined with a picnic.

A Reminder: For religious reasons, some parents wish to exclude their children from Easter activities. If this is true of any of your students, confine your activities to areas where there will be no objections. These will certainly include studies of anything in nature, and many language, math, and art projects.

AROUND
THE ROOM

ROOM DECORATIONS

EASTER EGG TREE

Materials: deep bucket filled with sand or pebbles, a bare tree branch, blown out egg shells (see page 76), Easter egg dye, yarn or string, long craft needle.

1. Put the tree branch into the bucket. Use the sand or pebbles in the bucket to support the tree branch and to hold it in place.

2. Dye the blown out egg shells. Dry.

3. To attach string or yarn to egg, thread the string through a long craft needle. (A teacher's aide may need to help with this step.) Tie a knot at the end of the string. Draw the needle through the egg so that the knot goes through one end hole but not the other hole. Remove needle.

4. Hang the dyed shells from the tree branch.

Variation: Have a theme for your tree, perhaps based on a unit you've been studying in social studies or science. See illustration for examples.

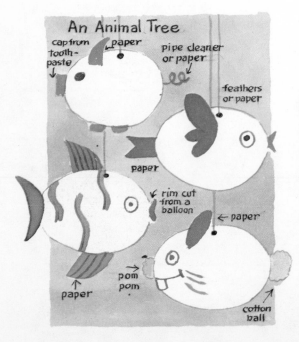

YARN EGGS

Note: This project sounds messy. It is. But it is fun and creative for the children. The eggs can be kept for many years.

Materials: balloons, string, long pieces of brightly-colored yarn, liquid starch or white glue, and water.

1. Blow up balloons into egg shapes, and tie them tightly so no air can get out. Tie a length of string on each balloon so it can be hung up later.

2. Dip long pieces of yarn in a solution of half liquid starch or white glue and half water.

3. Wrap pieces of wet yarn around balloon in all directions.

4. Balloons may either be hung up to dry, or laid on sheets of waxed paper. Dry them thoroughly.

5. When the yarn is dry, it will be hard and stiff. Prick the balloon with a pin. Gently remove the pieces of balloon from inside the egg-shaped yarn.

6. Hang the eggs from the classroom ceiling. A pretty bow may be tied on the balloon string if desired. If enough space is left in between the yarn strips, some green Easter grass may be gently dropped in the bottom of the egg.

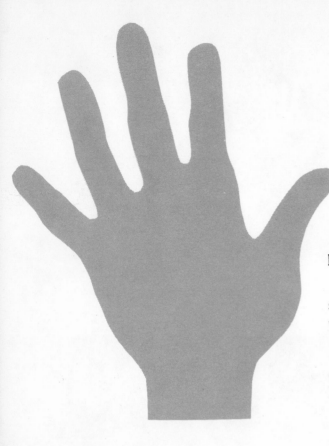

HAND PRINT EASTER LILIES

Materials: white paper, pencil, scissors, transparent tape, 9" x 12" yellow construction paper, crayons.

1. With pencil, trace around child's hand on white paper. Fingers should be spread out.

2. Let each child cut out his traced hand shape. Roll into cone with base of pinky meeting and overlapping base of thumb. Tape to hold shape. Curl each finger gently backwards. This may be done by rolling the paper around a pencil or the child's thumb.

3. Tape to construction paper. Draw stem and leaves with green crayon.

4. Print "Happy Easter" or "Happy Spring" at bottom of the construction paper. Hang on walls of room or hallway.

Note: This project not only makes a good room or hallway decoration, it is also a keepsake of the child's hand size at that age.

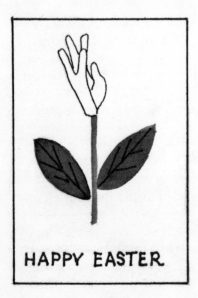

HAPPY EASTER

TISSUE-PAPER BUTTERFLIES

Materials: different colors of tissue paper, clip-type clothespins, black chenille wires.

1. Using the pattern on this page, cut two pieces of tissue paper (different shades or colors) in the shape of butterfly wings.

2. Clip the tissue paper together, between the wings, with a clip-style clothespin as the butterfly body.

3. Bend a chenille wire in half and curve each end. Clip the chenille wire with the clothespin to serve as antennae.

4. Clip butterflies to wires stretched across the room, or suspend them from the ceiling in groups near the windows.

SPRING KITES

Materials: bright colors of 9" x 12" construction paper, scissors, crayons or paint, string, crepe paper, stapler and staples.

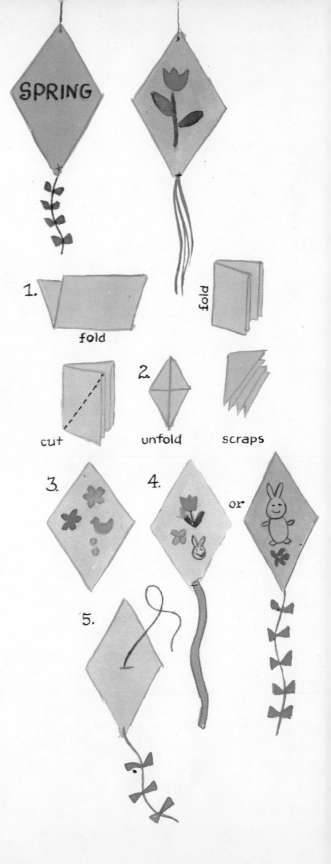

1. Fold a sheet of the construction paper in half. Fold in half again.

2. Cut diagonally from folded corner to folded corner. Unfold your diamond-shaped kite.

3. Decorate kite with paint, crayons or paper scraps.

4. With a stapler, add a tail made from crepe paper.

5. Staple a length of string to the middle of the kite and hang from ceiling.

Variations: A. Instead of decorating the kite, have each child suggest a spring word to write on his kite.

B. Instead of using crepe paper for a tail, older children may staple a length of string to the kite. Tie three or four 1" x 4" strips of crepe paper around the string.

20

BULLETIN BOARDS

ANIMAL WAKE-UP TIME

Materials: blue, brown, and white paper; pictures of animals that hibernate.

1. Cover the top half of bulletin board with blue paper for the sky. Cover the bottom half with brown paper cut to resemble rolling hills. Make flaps in the brown paper.

2. From more brown paper cut out the shape of a tree stump. Place in center of bulletin board, resting on ground.

3. Write across top or attach cut-out letters: "Animal Wake-Up Time. Peek Inside!"

4. Cut a strip of white paper representing snow to cover the brown ground.

5. Tape or tack pictures of hibernating animals under the flaps in the brown ground. Suggestions: bear, badger, snake, skunk, dormouse, porcupine, chipmunk, groundhog, squirrel, bat, toad, frog.

6. Allow times for the children to peek under the flaps. Talk about how the animals prepare to hibernate, the slow-down of bodily processes, and the waking up process.

ANIMAL EASTER PARADE

Materials: light blue and green paper, imitation grass, cotton balls, glue or tape, 9" x 12" construction paper in white and bright colors, crayons or felt markers, sequins and/or glitter, patterns of chicks, lambs, peacocks, and butterflies.

Note: The teacher may need to make sturdy cardboard patterns using the animal shapes on this page.

1. Cover top half of bulletin board with light blue paper. Cover bottom half with green paper cut to resemble rolling hills. Attach imitation grass along bottom. Glue or tape cotton balls in the sky for clouds.

2. Print or use cut-out letters across sky for title: "Animal Easter Parade."

3. Let the children trace around the animal patterns onto construction paper. They, or an aide, may cut out the animals and decorate them with crayons or felt markers. Glue sequins and/or glitter on the butterflies and peacocks. Glue cotton balls on the lambs.

4. Pin or tape animals on the board. Place the chicks, lambs, and peacocks in the grass and on the green hills. Place the butterflies among the cotton-ball clouds in the sky.

THE READING RABBIT

Materials: light blue paper, white construction paper, scissors, crayons or felt-tipped markers, green plastic Easter grass, construction paper in bright colors, stapler, cardboard egg-shaped pattern.

1. Cover the bulletin board with light blue paper.

2. Staple a 6", green, construction paper border to the bottom of the bulletin board. Gently stuff green Easter grass between the border and the bulletin board.

3. Make a bunny out of 2 white construction paper circles. The head should be about 7" in diameter, the body about 9". With crayons or felt-tipped markers, draw eyes, nose, mouth, and whiskers on the head circle. Four small circles may be drawn on the body for feet. Cut long ears out of the left-over white paper. Tape or glue the parts together.

4. Make a book for the bunny to read out of a 3" x 4" piece of brightly-colored construction paper. Fold paper in half, print a title and author's name on the front cover, and tape lower corners to rabbit's forefeet.

5. Attach the rabbit to the bulletin board so that he is standing in the middle of the grass. (A rabbit could be drawn directly onto the light blue paper instead of making one out of construction paper. A store-bought bunny could also be used.)

6. Print or use cut-out letters to add the title at the top of the bulletin board: "The Reading Rabbit."

7. Ask the children to read as many books as possible. Place a cardboard egg-shaped pattern and construction paper in a convenient place. Each time a child reads a story, have him cut out an egg shape from construction paper. Print the book title and author on the egg and put the egg on the bulletin board in the grass.

HOPPIN' DOWN THE BUNNY TRAIL

Materials: light green and light brown paper, white and tan construction paper, green Easter grass.

1. Several weeks before you will be using them, ask each child to bring a wallet-sized photo of his family to school.

2. Cover the bulletin board with light green paper. Make a trail diagonally across the board using the light brown paper.

3. Print or use cut-out letters for the title: "Hoppin' Down the Bunny Trail."

4. Give each child a sheet of 9" x 12" white construction paper. Have each child draw and cut out a bunny. (A snowman with long ears makes a good front view of a bunny.)

5. Give each child a piece of 4½" x 6" tan construction paper to make a basket for the bunny to hold. Tape the basket to the front of the bunny, leaving the top part free.

6. Have each child slip his family photo into the basket. If a photo is not available, have the child draw a small picture of his family on an egg-shaped piece of paper.

7. Pin or tape the bunnies to the bulletin board. Add green Easter grass along the trail, if desired.

8. Discuss families and how they grow and mature, just as plants grow in the springtime.

LEARNING CENTERS

SHAPE-UP EGGS

This learning center is geared specifically for kindergarteners and first grade students. It will help them learn shapes and develop small muscle coordination.

To set up this activity, you will need to provide drawing paper, crayons, scissors, and four oak tag or cardboard egg shapes. In the center of one egg cut out a rectangle; in another cut a square; in the third cut a triangle; in the last cut a circle.

Explain to the children that when they visit this center, they should place a piece of paper behind an egg shape and then trace the shape inside the egg, color it, and cut it out.

If you have an aide or teacher's helper, have him or her stationed in the learning center so that when a child finishes all the shapes, he can tell the aide what shapes he has made. Encourage the children to tell their parents at home also.

SPRINGTIME JOURNAL

Second graders and advanced first graders will enjoy this creative writing project. It will help sharpen their observation skills, and develop vocabulary and writing ability.

For this learning center you will need to provide writing paper, 12" x 18" construction paper (one brightly-colored sheet for each child), crayons or felt-tipped markers, stapler.

Tell the class what a journal is. Explain the instructions below to the entire class. Then post the directions in the learning center so that students can work there independently.

1. Fold the construction paper in half.

2. Put several sheets of writing paper inside.

3. Staple together on the folded side to make a book-like journal.

4. Use crayons or markers to decorate the cover.

5. Write about Easter or springtime things. (Write about the buds and blossoms on trees and bushes; about sprouting flowers and grass; about nests or eggs, birds, and other animals; about the weather. Write about what you see, hear, smell, taste, and feel.)

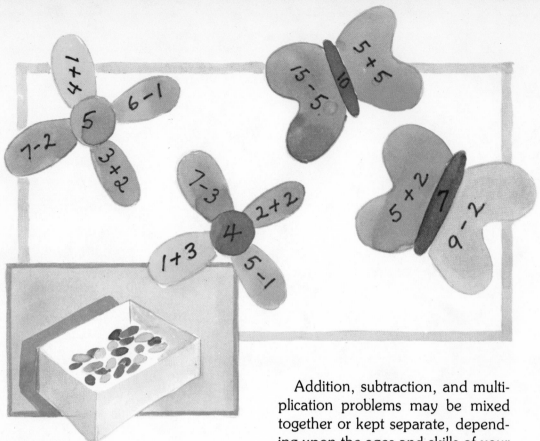

Addition, subtraction, and multiplication problems may be mixed together or kept separate, depending upon the ages and skills of your students.

You may want to station an aide in this center to offer assistance to the students.

Variations: A. Math butterflies. On the cut-out butterfly bodies, print the math problems. Have the children match the wings to the correct body.

B. For younger children, print numbers on the circles but use blank petals. Instruct the children to make a flower using the amount of petals that corresponds to the number on the circle. That is, three petals will be used to make the flower with the number 3 in the circle.

SPRING MATH FLOWERS

This learning center idea can help your students practice and improve their math skills.

You will need to provide construction paper circles and petal shapes, and a box in which to keep the circles and petals.

To prepare the center for student visitation, print a number on each circle, and print a math problem on each petal.

Instruct the children to make flowers by matching the problem petals to the correct answer written on a circle.

SPRING GARDEN

Since spring is the time for new life and growth, provide an opportunity for your students to plant some seeds and watch them grow.

For this center, you'll need to provide styrofoam cups, potting soil, lettuce or other quick growing seeds, sprinkling can, and water.

You'll want to explain this procedure to the class as a whole and also post the directions in the learning center so students can work there independently, or with the assistance of an aide.

DIRECTIONS
1. Put soil in a cup—about 3".

2. Make a little hole in the dirt with your finger and drop the seeds in the hole.

3. Barely cover the seeds with soil.

4. *Sprinkle* the soil with water so the seeds are not washed out of place.

5. Place cup near a window.

6. Keep soil damp, but not soaked.

Note: Placing a piece of plastic wrap over the top of the cup will speed germination. When sprouts appear, the plastic should be removed.

Variation: For older children, keep a garden calendar. Note on the calendar the day the seeds were planted, the day of the first sprout, the height of the plants from day to day, etc.

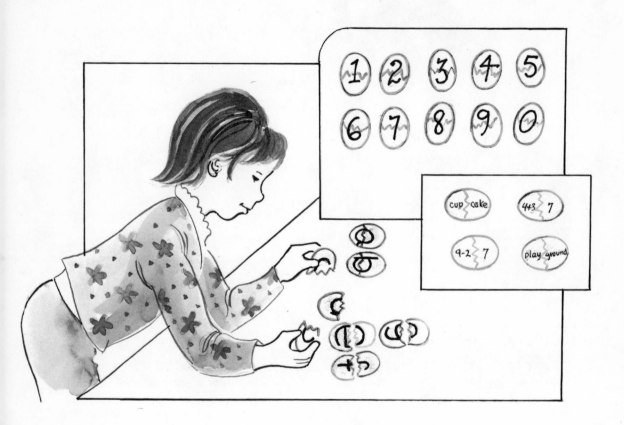

EASTER EGG MATCH-UP

This simple-to-set-up learning center will enable your students to work independently on identifying letters and numbers.

For this center you will need thirty-six egg shapes cut from brightly-colored construction paper. Print a letter of the alphabet on each of twenty-six eggs. Print a numeral from 0 to 9 on each of the other ten eggs. Cut each egg into two puzzle-like pieces. Mix the pieces.

Tell the children ahead of time that when they visit the center, they are to put the correct pieces together, and then separate the letters from the numbers. Demonstrate the procedure before the entire class, but allow the children to attend the center individually or in pairs.

EASTER EGGS IN WATER

Kindergarten and first grade children will especially enjoy experimenting in this center. This activity will help students determine what floats and what sinks in water.

Materials needed for this center include plastic eggs; small objects of various weights, such as stones, feathers, cotton balls, wooden thread spools, cork, buttons, coins, etc.; dishpan or oblong cake pan; and water.

Set up a table in a corner of the room with the materials. Fill the pan with water.

Explain to the students that when they visit the center they should find out which objects float and which ones sink. Explain the procedure to the class as a whole before letting students independently visit the center.

Here is the procedure.

Place an object into an egg, and then put the egg into the water. Observe what happens. Then put the object directly into the water. Test the other objects.

After everyone has had a chance to visit the center, discuss the activity. Have the children tell you what happened to each object inside and outside the egg. Talk about the differences.

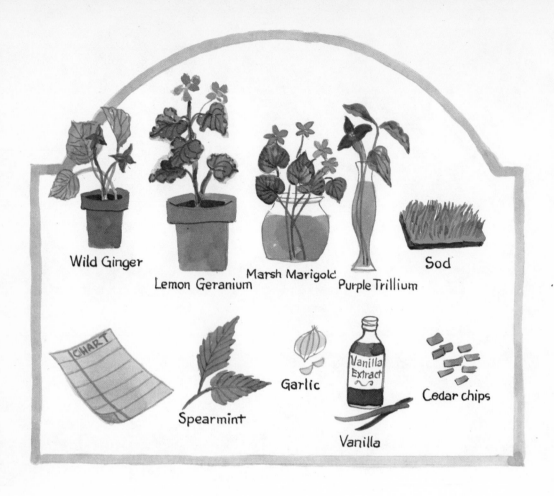

Wild Ginger

Lemon Geranium

Marsh Marigold

Purple Trillium

Sod

CHART

Spearmint

Garlic

Vanilla
Extract

Vanilla

Cedar chips

SCENT STATION

Let your students enjoy the smells of spring. Set up a "scent" learning center in your classroom. Have second and third grade students sniff, detect, and record the smells.

You'll need a table, a chart for students to record their findings, and a collection of smelly plants— sweet smelling flowers, freshly cut grass, leaves from spearmint plants, lemon geranium; and also things such as vanilla beans or extract, garlic cloves, cedar chips, etc.

GAMES
AND RHYTHMIC
ACTIVITIES

LEARNING GAMES

Purposes: The following games are suggested to foster development of math comprehension and for drilling math facts.

EGGS IN THE CARTON

Materials: an egg carton, twelve plastic eggs, marking pens, buttons, paper.

Procedure: Put twelve plastic eggs in the egg carton. Cover the top of the carton with paper. Do one of the following.

a. Put a number on the outside of each egg and put the same amount of buttons inside. Ask the children to take out the buttons from all of the eggs and then get the

correct amounts back inside.

b. Put corresponding dots on the bottom half of an egg and a written numeral on the top. Take the eggs apart, and ask the children to match the correct numerals with the dots.

c. Print a numeral on the outside of an egg and the same numeral on a piece of paper for the inside of it. Take all the papers out of the eggs, than get them all back in the correct places.

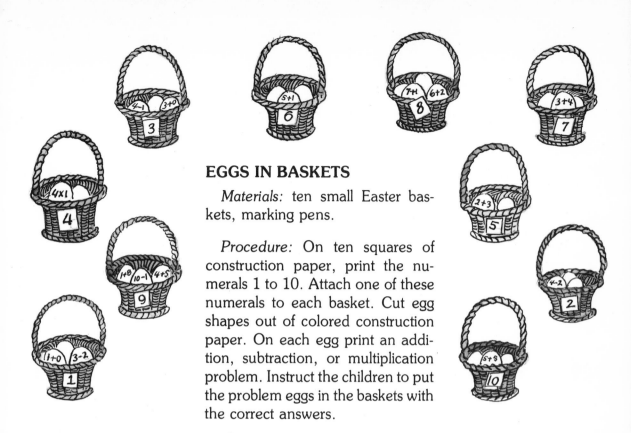

EGGS IN BASKETS

Materials: ten small Easter baskets, marking pens.

Procedure: On ten squares of construction paper, print the numerals 1 to 10. Attach one of these numerals to each basket. Cut egg shapes out of colored construction paper. On each egg print an addition, subtraction, or multiplication problem. Instruct the children to put the problem eggs in the baskets with the correct answers.

SPRING POND GAME

Materials: drawing paper, crayons or felt markers, one die or number cube.

Procedure: Explain the directions to the children. Two to four children may play at one time. Each player takes a sheet of drawing paper. Only roll the die or number cube once for each turn. Each player must roll a one to begin. When he gets a one, he draws a pond on his paper. Players continue to take turns, filling their ponds in the following sequence. On a roll of two, the player draws two ducks in his pond. When he rolls three, he draws three ducklings. When he gets four, he draws four frogs. On a roll of five, he adds five polliwogs. On a roll of six, he adds six fish. The first player to fill his pond wins the game.

Purpose: The following games are suggested for development of vocabulary and word recognition.

STEP INTO SPRING

Materials: construction paper, marking pen, scissors.

Procedure: Have the children trace around their shoes onto the construction paper. Cut out each shoe shape. Choose one spring word to write on each pair of shoe shapes. Mix up the shoe shapes. Take turns matching the words in pairs.

Variations: Write a compound word on each pair of shoes—half of the word on each shoe. Mix up the shoe shapes. Take turns combining the compound words.

FEED THE EASTER BUNNY

Materials: shoe box, white and orange construction paper, stapler, scissors or sharp knife, marking pen or crayon.

Procedure: On white construction paper, draw a large bunny face with a large smiling mouth. Cut out the face and two bunny ears. Staple the face and ears to the lid of the shoe box. With scissors or sharp knife, cut out the bunny's smiling mouth. Put the face-lid on the shoe box. From the orange construction paper, cut out carrot shapes. Print spring words on one side of the car-rot shapes. Stack the words face down beside the bunny. Any number of children may play the game at one time. To play, each player turns up one carrot on his turn. If he can read the word, he "feeds" it to the bunny. If he does not know the word, he returns it, face down, to the stack for the next player. If none of the players can read the word, put it face up on a separate pile. At the end of the game, the teacher or an aide helps the players learn the words in this pile. The object is to feed the Easter bunny all the car-rots.

RHYTHMIC ACTIVITIES

(Use the pattern on this page to cut out five pairs of little bunny ears. Tape the tabs together to fit your fingers. Put the ears on your finger tips to simulate bunnies. Hold up five fingers for the first verse, four fingers for the next verse, and so on, through the last verse.)

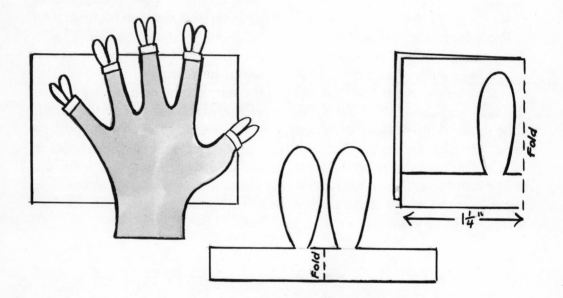

FIVE EASTER BUNNIES

Five Easter bunnies
  hopped to my door.
One came in to play with me.
  Then there were four.

Four Easter bunnies
  made an Easter-egg tree.
One brought it to my door,
  Then there were three.

Three Easter bunnies
  painted eggs for me and you.

One hid them in the garden.
  Then there were two.

Two Easter bunnies
  filled a basket. Oh! What fun.
One brought it to my door.
  Then there was one.

One Easter bunny
  said, "Happy Easter Day.
"I have lots of work to do."
  Then he hopped away.

by Jane Belk Moncure

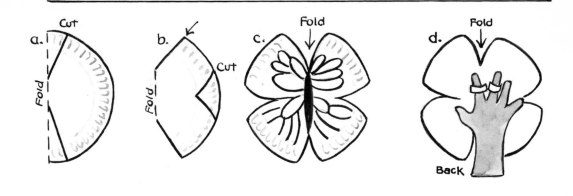

BUTTERFLY FINGER-PLAY PUPPET

Materials: paper plate, felt markers, scissors, two 2½" x ½" strips of oak tag or construction paper, transparent tape.

a. Fold paper plate in half. Close to the fold, cut about two inches from each end toward the center. Curve corners.

b. Cut V-shaped sections from middle of the rims toward the fold to form wings. Curve corners.

c. Draw butterfly body and wing markings with felt markers on front and back.

d. Make finger rings from both strips of oak tag. Tape onto back of butterfly at either side of fold. Use pointer and middle fingers to operate puppet.

I'm a little butterfly.
(Hold butterfly puppet in right hand.)
I spread my wings and fly so high!
(Spread butterfly wings and "fly.")
I look around until I see
A flower smiling up at me!
(Make flower shape with left hand.)

by Jane Belk Moncure

EASTER BUNNY

I heard the Easter bunny
   *(With right hand, form bunny
   ears with two fingers.)*
hop-hopping on the floor.
   (Make your bunny hop.)
He left my Easter basket
right beside the door.

I ran outside to catch him,
but guess what he did?
He hopped into a rabbit hole
   *(With left arm put hand on your
   hip and make a rabbit hole. Have
   your bunny hop in.)*
and hid! hid! hid!

by Jane Belk Moncure

THE BUTTERFLY

Brightly colored butterfly
Looking for honey,
Spread your wings and fly away
While it's still sunny.
   *(Place hands side by side —
   thumbs together — and wiggle fin-
   gers like the wings on a butterfly.)*

by Dotti Hannum

WELCOME SPRING

This is the sun so big and round.
(Put arms in a circle over head.)
This is a little bulb deep in the ground.
(Bend over and bring arms into knees.)
It reaches up and before you know,
(Start to pull up, arms still tucked in.)
Little shoots stretch out and start to grow.
(Reach arms up.)
Up, up they wiggle. Up, up they bring,
(Wiggle fingers and reach up.)
A pretty flower to welcome spring.
(Stretch arms straight up in the air.)

by Mae Kidman Aldous

SPRING IS HERE!

I heard it in the robin's song.
(Cup hands behind ears.)
I smelled its fragrance all day long.
(Lift nose and sniff.)
I felt it in the gentle rain.
(Flutter fingers downward.)
I saw it down the flowered lane.
(Put hand at foreheard. Peer ahead.)
The message came so loud and clear.
(Put hands at mouth as though calling.)
Spring is here! Spring is here!

by Beth Holzbauer

MOVE TO THE MUSIC

by Annetta Dellinger

Obtain a phonograph or tape recording of dance music—ballet, waltz, rumba, jazz, rock—any kind is fine. As the music plays, suggest the following movements.

1. Be a big egg, a small egg, a boiling egg bouncing in hot water, a scrambled egg.

2. Be a tiny chick in a shell, pecking your way out.

3. Be a bunny; march in the band in an Easter parade.

4. Crawl like a caterpillar; roll up in a cocoon; sleep; wake up; slowly unroll; shake out of the cocoon; flutter like a butterfly.

5. Be a farmer planting seeds in the ground; be a little seed under the ground and slowly grow up through the soil toward the sunshine.

THINGS
TO MAKE
AND DO

MAKE AN EASTER BASKET

Some families have the custom of making their own baskets and nests for the Easter bunny to fill with eggs. Children will enjoy making one of the following baskets. Decide what kind of baskets you will have the children make. Gather the supplies and explain the procedures.

1. *Milk carton basket.* Cut off the top of a clean and dry ½ pint milk carton saved from the child's lunch. Have child cover carton with construction paper, crepe paper, and/or stickers. Staple on a chenille wire, cardboard, or construction-paper handle.

1. Milk Carton Basket

2. *Bunny basket.* Remove the label from a cylindrical oatmeal box. Cut the middle section out of the top half of the box, leaving long flaps on each side that resemble rabbit ears. Decorate the box to look like a bunny face.

Optional: Thread a ribbon through holes punched near the tips of the ears. Bring the ears together, tie a bow, and use ears as a handle.

2. Bunny Bucket

3. *Salt box basket.* (Each salt box will make two baskets.) Cut a cylindrical salt box in half. Cover each half with construction paper. Decorate with paints, crayons, or stickers. Attach a cardboard or chenille wire handle with staples.

3. Salt Box Basket

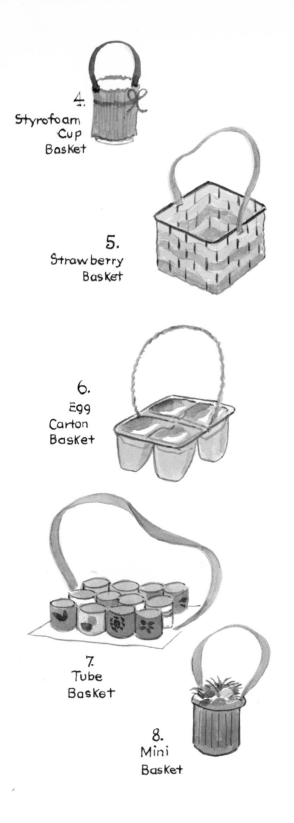

4. Styrofoam Cup Basket

5. Strawberry Basket

6. Egg Carton Basket

7. Tube Basket

8. Mini Basket

4. *Styrofoam cup basket.* Wrap crepe paper around cup. Tie with yarn around middle. Staple a length of ribbon to top for a handle.

5. *Strawberry basket.* Weave pastel-colored ribbon through a plastic strawberry basket. Tie a length of ribbon on two sides for the handle.

6. *Egg carton basket.* Cut a 4-section portion from a styrofoam egg carton. For a handle, stick the ends of a 12-inch chenille wire through opposite sides of the basket. Fold up the tips of the chenille wire to secure it.

7. *Tube basket.* Cut four to twelve paper-roll tubes into 2 to 3-inch sections. Staple or paper clip sides together in a cluster. Glue the cluster onto a stiff cardboard base. Decorate with paint (spray paint works well), crayons, paper, or stickers. Staple on a length of ribbon or chenille wire for a handle.

8. *Mini-basket.* Use a clean, large bottle cap, such as comes on a liquid fabric softener bottle. Glue on a length of ¼" ribbon for a handle. On a mini-nest of plastic grass, place jelly-bean eggs.

EASTER GIFTS AND FAVORS

Easter is a time for giving gifts and for having parties. Some of the following ideas make nice gifts. Some make favors for parties, Easter dinner, or a spring festival. Some of the projects would be suitable for either gifts or favors.

EASTER CORSAGE

Materials: a 5" paper doily, flower (single silk rose is best), ribbon, stapler, safety pins.

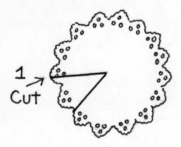

1. Cut out a 1/6 wedge from doily.

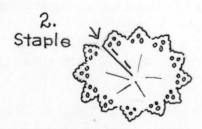

2. Bring doily together where it was cut. Gather and fold doily so complete circle is formed and it has a gathered, lacy effect. Staple doily in center to maintain gathers.

3. Tie ribbon around flower and into a bow.

4. Attach flower to doily background (staple or pin in inconspicuous place).

5. Put safety pin on back so it can be worn. The corsage makes a nice gift for Mom.

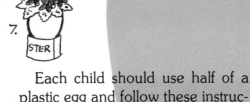

EGG EASTER SCENE

Materials: plastic egg-shaped hosiery container, small paper doily, poster board, markers or crayons, rickrack, Easter grass, plastic or silk flowers, glue, scissors.

CATERPILLAR

Materials: a strip of paper 9" x 1½", eight strips of paper 5" x 1½", glue or paste, felt marker, chenille wire.

1. Glue ends of each 5" x 1½" strip together to form a circle.

2. Glue the circles to the 9" x 1½" base strip.

3. Draw a smiling face on the head circle with the marker.

4. Cut two feelers, each about 1½" long, from the chenille wire. Stick ends into the head circle and bend.

5. Attach a string at the front of the base strip for a pull toy. Give to a younger sister or brother.

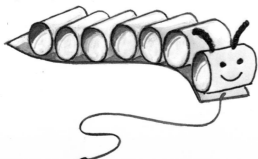

Each child should use half of a plastic egg and follow these instructions.

1. Glue rickrack on egg's edge.

2. Push doily into egg to use for background. Glue if necessary.

3. Put Easter grass in egg.

4. Put flower(s) in egg. Variation: have Easter bunny and eggs in the scene.

5. Using the poster board, cut out egg stand (see pattern). Cut slits as marked.

6. Color the egg stand if desired. Print an Easter message on it (Happy Easter). Join the stand together at slits with ends inside.

7. Put your egg on the stand to display it.

EGG PERSON

Materials: a 2" styrofoam egg; chenille wire; moving eyes, if desired; scraps of yarn and felt; glue; scissors; pins.

1. Tell the children they are to create an "egg person."

2. Each child may cut two 3-inch pieces of chenille wire for the arms. Bend the wire into circles for the hands, and stick into opposite sides of the egg.

3. To make the creation stand up, form a 6" length of chenille wire into a heart shape, leaving ends at the "v" to stick into the egg. Bend egg forward if it is off-balanced.

4. To make the hair, instruct the children to cut 3" pieces of yarn and tie them together in the center with a piece of yarn. The hair can be attached to the egg with a pin.

5. The children may cut out facial features from felt scraps. Glue or pin these onto the egg. Or glue on moving eyes.

CHICK IN THE EGG

Materials: cotton balls, individual cups cut from egg cartons, yellow tempera paint or felt markers, black felt marker, glue, orange paper scraps, scissors.

1. Tint the cotton balls with the yellow tempera paint or felt markers.

2. Glue the tinted cotton balls into the cups cut from egg cartons.

3. Draw eyes on the cotton ball using the black felt marker.

4. Cut out a beak from the orange paper scraps. Glue it to the cotton ball.

Variation: Instead of egg-carton cups, use carefully broken egg-shell halves that have been rinsed and dried. Glue a white life-saver to the outside of the egg shell for a base.

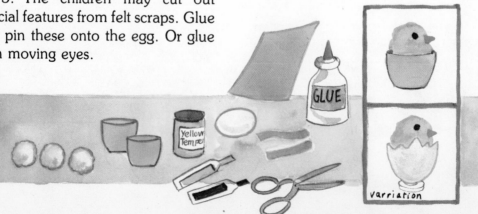

varriation

BUNNY CUP

Materials: individual cups cut from white egg cartons, construction paper scraps, scissors, glue, felt markers.

1. Cut the rabbit's ears, eyes, nose, and mouth from construction paper scraps. Glue them onto an egg-carton cup.

2. Draw whiskers with a felt marker.

3. Fill the cup with candy to use as favor, or with jelly to go on Easter breakfast toast.

NUTTY FLOWER BASKET

Materials: walnut shell, halved; very small dried flowers (straw flowers), chenille wire, glue, modeling clay, scissors.

1. Cut a 4-inch piece of chenille wire for the handle. Glue to the inside of the shell at each end. Don't use the handle until the glue is completely dry.

2. Fill bottom of shell with modeling clay. Push the clay firmly around the chenille wire to further secure the handle.

3. Fill basket with flowers by pushing the flower stems into the clay. For best results, put flowers in one at a time or tape a bunch together before putting them into the clay. When the clay hardens, the basket may be used as a favor for the spring festival. It would also look pretty hanging on an Easter-egg tree, or it could be given as a gift.

COOKIE POP

Materials: a round sugar cookie baked on a dowel stick, scraps of construction paper, frosting in tubes, frosting decorating tips, two chocolate chips or raisins, a piece of red cinnamon candy, ribbon, empty thread spool, fine-line felt marker.

1. Make rabbit ears from construction paper. Attach them to cookie with dabs of frosting.

2. Use chocolate chips or raisins for eyes, cinnamon candy for nose. Attach with dabs of frosting.

3. Draw whiskers and mouth with frosting.

4. Tie a length of ribbon or yarn into a bow around the stick.

5. Print "Happy Easter" on spool. Place stick in hole of spool and stand in place.

BUNNY NAPKIN HOLDER

Materials: an 11" x 1¼" strip of construction paper or ribbon, white felt, cotton balls, moving eyes or small beads, fine-point black marker, stapler, glue, scissors.

1. Loop front of ribbon (or paper) forming bunny head. Staple loop at bottom.

2. Loop back of ribbon forward, forming bunny body (should be larger than head). Staple loop at bottom.

3. From felt, cut out bunny feet and bunny ears (see patterns).

4. Glue feet under head. Glue ears in back of head.

5. Glue cotton ball on for tail.

6. Glue on eyes to make face.

7. Draw on bunny nose, mouth, and whiskers with marker.

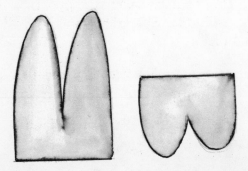

GROWING FLOWERS

Start this project early enough so that the plants will be ready by spring vacation. They would make nice Easter gifts.

Materials: plastic egg cartons, potting soil, marigold seeds (or other fast-growing seeds), large eye dropper, scissors.

1. Cut the egg cartons into individual cups, and give one cup to each child. Have each child put his initials on the bottom of his cup.

2. Let each child fill his cup with soil (about 2 teaspoons) and gently place several seeds just under the soil.

3. Put the cups on plastic-lined cookie sheets placed near a window.

4. Children may take turns watering the plants, using the eye dropper. Caution them not to over-water the plants.

BUNNY PRETZELS

Ingredients: a pkg. active dry yeast, 1½ cups warm water, 1 teaspoon salt, 1 tablespoon sugar, 4 cups flour, a beaten egg, coarse salt.

1. Dissolve yeast in warm water.

2. Add remaining ingredients. Mix.

3. Knead until smooth. Add up to 1 cup more flour if dough is sticky.

4. Divide dough into walnut-sized pieces. Give one to each child.

5. Roll each ball into a rope 12" to 14" long. Shape into an Easter bunny.

6. Brush with beaten egg. Sprinkle with coarse salt.

7. Bake at 425° F. for 15 to 18 minutes.

BUBBLING

Easter is a time when the weather is getting nice and little things begin to grow bigger. Make some bubble mix, and watch those little bubbles grow bigger and bigger and fly away in the spring breeze.

Mix 1 tablespoon of dish detergent, 2 tablespoons of water and 4 drops of corn syrup for the basic mix. Now try wire whisks, slotted spoons, hand cheese graters, plastic 6-pack holders, embroidery hoops, bent paper clips, etc., as the dippers. If you add glycerine and a pinch of sugar to the solution, you can create giant bubbles. (Glycerine may be obtained from a drug store.) Food coloring can also be added to the water. If mix is put into a dishpan, wire coat hangers can be shaped into Easter bunnies and used as the bubble dippers.

SONGS AND POEMS

Little Bunny, Come My Way

P.L.G.

Paulette Lutz Glenn

1. Lit - tle bun - ny, hop! hop! hop! Bring - ing Eas - ter eggs, please, don't stop! Don't de - lay! It's Eas - ter Day! Lit - tle bun - ny, come my way!

2. Lit - tle bun - ny, stop to see All good chil-dren, in - clud - ing me! Bring - ing toys for girls and boys, Ver - y spe - cial Eas - ter joys!

Note: This song is a "bunny-hop"! Form a line with each child's hands on shoulders of person ahead of him. Hop with feet together in the following manner.

Hop forward (freeze). Hop backward (freeze). Hop forward Hop forward Hop forward.

Lit	tle	bun	ny,	hop!	hop!	hop!
Bring	ing	Easter	eggs,	please,	don't	stop!
Don't	de	lay!	It's	Eas	ter	Day!
Lit	tle	bun	ny,	come	my	way!

(Same manner on 2nd verse.)

New Babies

P.L.G.

Paulette Lutz Glenn

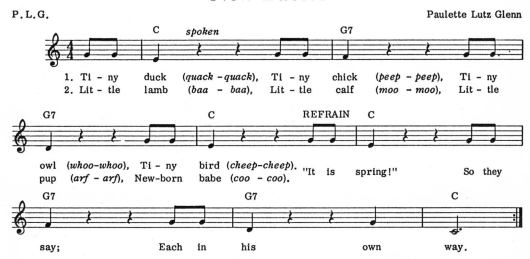

1. Ti - ny duck (*quack - quack*), Ti - ny chick (*peep - peep*), Ti - ny
2. Lit - tle lamb (*baa - baa*), Lit - tle calf (*moo - moo*), Lit - tle

owl (*whoo-whoo*), Ti - ny bird (*cheep-cheep*). "It is spring!" So they
pup (*arf - arf*), New-born babe (*coo - coo*).

say; Each in his own way.

Note: A few children might play some small, quiet rhythm instruments such as jingle bells or a triangle or rhythm sticks to accompany this song. Or during the rests in the refrain, have the children pat their knees for a quiet accompaniment.

Wake Up!

R.M.P.

Ruth Morgan Powell

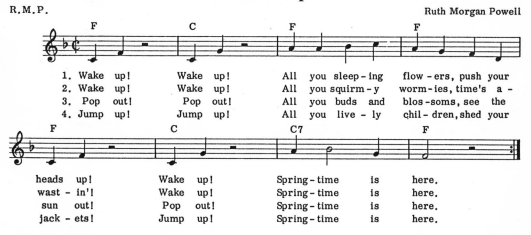

1. Wake up!   Wake up!   All you sleep - ing   flow - ers, push your
2. Wake up!   Wake up!   All you squirm - y   worm - ies, time's a -
3. Pop out!   Pop out!   All you buds and   blos - soms, see the
4. Jump up!   Jump up!   All you live - ly   chil - dren, shed your

heads up!   Wake up!   Spring - time is here.
wast - in'!   Wake up!   Spring - time is here.
sun out!   Pop out!   Spring - time is here.
jack - ets!   Jump up!   Spring - time is here.

Note: This song lends itself to having children make up their own verses to the song. Also, children can accompany themselves with the tone bells C and F played in time on the appropriate measures. Simple F and C octaves on the piano make a very effective and easy accompaniment.

Rabbity Ears

R.M.P.

Ruth Morgan Powell

1. Oh, it's no trou-ble for a kid like me To
2. Oh, my own ears are small and flat.

wig-gle my nose so hap-pi-ly. And I can eat car-rots with a
Most folks are happy with ears like that! And though I look just like a

great big crunch, Or hop to the ta-ble when it's time for lunch; But
per-son should, I'd like to be a bun-ny an-y time I could. But

me, oh, my, I'm far from glad, There's one more thing I wish I had:
car-rot, or not, as you can see, With-out those ears I'm just plain me!

CHORUS: In a swingin', blues style

Rab-bit-y ears! Rab-bit-y ears! I could hear ev-'ry-thing a bun - ny____ hears.____ And I would be so hap - py ____ in - side, my dears, If I could on - ly have some rab-bit-y ears!

DID YOU EVER SEE A BUNNY?

An action poem that can be sung to the tune of "Did You Ever See a Lassie?"

Did you ever see a bunny, a bunny, a bunny?
Did you ever see a bunny that hops so slow?
He hops and hops and hops and hops.
Did you ever see a bunny that hops so slow?

Additional verses: hops so fast
hops backwards
hops in a circle
hops on one foot

Did you ever see a duck, a duck, a duck?
Did you ever see a duck that waddles so slow?
He waddles and waddles and waddles and waddles.
Did you ever see a duck that waddles so slow?

Additional verses: waddles so fast
waddles backwards
waddles in a circle

by Annetta Dellinger

EASTER

Easter bunny goes hop, hop, hop;
Fills our baskets to the top.
Baby chicks cry peep, peep, peep.
Pretty flowers, up they creep.

Easter is a joyous day;
Time for fun, and time to play;
Time to share, and time to sing.
Easter says hello to spring.

by Patricia Stone Martin

SPRING IS HERE TODAY

I don't have to put my boots on,
Mittens, scarf, or hat.
All I need now is a sweater,
And a ball and bat.

There are no more little snowflakes
Landing on my nose.
Jack Frost isn't even busy
Freezing up my toes.

Breezes now are soft and gentle—
It is time to play.
All the world is brightly saying,
Spring is here today.

by Patricia Stone Martin

EASTER EGGS

Easter eggs are prettier
Than any I have seen.
One is red and one is blue,
And one is white and green.

by Dotti Hannum

SPRING

The sun keeps me warm from head
    to toe,
I hope that it will never go.

by Dotti Hannum

WAKE UP!

Wake up! Wake up! It's time for
    spring.
Can you hear the robins sing?
Caterpillar nods her head.
Oh, she wants to stay in bed!
Wake up! Wake up! It's very clear,
Winter's gone, and spring is here!

by Mae Kidman Aldous

WHO AM I?

SPRING RIDDLES

by Mae Kidman Aldous

You see me on flowers.
Sometimes I fly.
You can guess who I am,
If you'll only try.
I have to admit
Some are afraid of me.
I am yellow and black.
You call me a_____.

I always return
When it is spring.
You'll find me hunting
For twigs and string.
I won't be held,
But I'll be heard.
I get up early.
You call me a_____.

If you look closely,
You'll have to agree.
It's hard to tell which end
Is the head of me.
If you pick me up,
I'll wiggle and squirm.
I live underground.
You call me a_____.

I like to hop.
I like to eat.
I think strawberries
Are a special treat.
I have big ears.
Some say they are funny.
You see me at Easter.
You call me a_____.

I like to walk,
Or trot, or run.
If you ride on me,
You'll have some fun.
Do I like oats?
Yes, of course.
I like to race.
You call me a_____.

I'm not very big.
I run very fast.
When I run in a hole,
My tail will be last.
When it gets very cold,
I want in the house.
I love to eat cheese.
You call me a_____.

Answers: bee, bird, worm, bunny, horse, mouse.

A
SPRING
FESTIVAL

Fun! Laughter! Games! Food! Singing! Dancing! All of these make a festival. Spring is a time of joy — a season to celebrate. Having a spring festival can provide a wonderful celebration. Whether small and simple or big and elaborate, the key to success is remembering that festivals are to be enjoyed. With that in mind, the following suggestions are offered for use and adaptation.

DECORATIONS

The festival may be held in one or more classrooms, hallways, larger assembly areas, or outdoors. Any of these places may already have seasonal decorations. (See pages 16-20.) The activities planned will determine some decorations. Balloons add a festive touch to any setting, besides which you may wish to hang crepe-paper streamers in pastel colors and/or flower garlands.

GAMES

Choose from the following ideas. Learning games may be found on pages 34-37.

PASS THE BASKET RELAY

Equipment: a basket and plastic eggs for each team.

Procedure: Divide the children into teams of equal number with approximately six on a team. The players stand in a line, about a foot apart. The first player on each team is given a basket. When this relay is first played, the basket should be empty, but when the pupils learn how to do it, they will have more fun if there are eggs in the basket. At the signal, "Get ready, go!" the first player passes the basket over his head to player two without turning. Player two passes the basket between his legs to player three. Player three passes the basket over his head to player four, etc., until the last person in line gets the basket. He, then, moves to the front of the line and passes the basket over his head to the previous player one, who passes the basket between his legs to the next person in line. This process continues until all players have had opportunity to be first in line. The team that returns to starting order first is the winner.

EGG-N-SPOON RELAY

Equipment: a spoon and a plastic egg (or ping-pong ball) for each team.

Procedure: Divide players into teams of equal number, with six to ten children for each team. Mark a beginning point in front of the first person on each team. At least twenty feet away, mark the turning point. The first person on each team is given the egg in the spoon. At the signal, "Get set, go!" the first person walks rapidly to the turning point and back, without dropping the egg. If the egg is dropped, the player who dropped it must pick it up and go back to the point where he dropped it, then continue to complete his turn. When the carrier crosses the beginning point, he hands the egg in the spoon to the next player, etc. The team which completes two turns first is the winner.

Variation: As the players become more experienced, the egg carrier might be required to hold his free hand behind his back, not using it for any reason. He would be allowed to use his foot, or the fingers of the hand in which he is carrying the spoon if he needs to replace the dropped egg.

CANIGELN

Equipment: a hard-boiled egg for each child, a croquet wicket or similar arch.

Procedure: Place a croquet wicket or similar arch several feet away from a line. Let each child stand at the line and, in turn, try to roll his egg (as in bowling) through the wicket. Cracking an eggshell disqualifies the player. Whoever gets an unbroken egg through the wicket is a winner.

BUNNY RABBIT RELAY

Equipment: none.

Procedure: Divide the children into teams of no more than ten each. Draw a line for the beginning point and have the teams line up behind that line. Mark a turning point twenty feet or more from that point.

The first child on each team squats, holding his ankles. At the command, "On you mark, get set, go!" the child will jump, continuing to hold his ankles, to the turning point and back. When he crosses the beginning point, the next person on his team will begin jumping. This procedure will continue until each child in the group has completed the distance.

You may choose to have the winner be the team which is first to complete two or three turns.

Variations: Such a relay may be done using any locomotive movements which are appropriate for the development of the child.

Examples: Galloping—pretend to be a pony. Hopping—hold one foot at front or back. Jumping—keep feet close together. Skiping—low and/or high skip. Sliding—pretend to be a trombone. Running—pretend to be a deer.

EGG HUNT

Equipment: colored, hard-boiled eggs, and/or candy eggs wrapped in paper; a container for each child in which to put his eggs.

Procedure: Before the festival, hide eggs in room or yard. At the "Go!" signal, the children look for the eggs, putting them in their containers when they find them. The hunt may stop when all the eggs are found or when an allotted amount of time has passed. Each child keeps the eggs he finds.

Variations: 1. Prepare six eggs for each child. Print the letters E-A-S-T-E-R or S-P-R-I-N-G on each set of six eggs. Hide them. Each child must find a set. Children may help each other.

2. Write numbers on the eggs. Add up the numbers at the end of the hunt and the largest (or smallest) score wins.

DRAMAS

Including a play in the Spring Festival can add to the fun. The following are two possibilities you may want to consider doing.

A SPRING GARDEN PARADE

by Mae Kidman Aldous

Note to the teacher: This play may have as few as nine or ten characters. Or you may include any number of children as Raindrops or Vegetables.

Simple costumes are recommended. Farmer Brown could wear a farmer's hat. Mrs. Brown needs only an apron over regular school clothes. For the Sun, have the actor paint a picture of a large sun on paper. This may be taped to the child's clothes or held in his hands. Likewise, the actors playing the parts of Raindrops could paint pictures of raindrops on poster paper. Each poster may be hung around the neck by attaching a string; it may be taped to the child's clothing; or it may be held in the child's hands. Allow each child who plays the part of a Vegetable to paint a poster of his favorite vegetable. These posters will be worn or held as are those of the Raindrops. Be sure the Vegetables include stringbeans, carrots, tomatoes, beets, and yellow potatoes.

CHARACTERS: Farmer Brown, Mrs. Brown, Sun, Raindrops, Vegetables.

PROP: a cardboard box with lid. Printed prominently on the side are the words, "Magical Garden Seeds."

SETTING: outdoors on Farmer Brown's farm, in early spring.

(The children who have painted vegetable posters are pretending to be asleep with their posters face down on the floor.)

(Enter Farmer Brown and Mrs. Brown.)

FARMER BROWN: Spring is coming! There's going to be a parade. I've got to get ready.

MRS. BROWN: Where's your magical seed box?

FARMER BROWN: I don't know. Have you seen it? *(Looks for box.)*

MRS. BROWN: Here it is. It's full of spring magic. *(Takes box to Farmer Brown.)*

FARMER BROWN: *(Lifts box lid. Takes out imaginary seeds and sprinkles over sleeping Vegetables.)*

A sprinkle here, a sprinkle there,
Is just the magic I need.
Then I say to one and all,
Grow, each little seed.

Now I need some helpers.

SUN: I will bring you sunshine.

RAINDROPS: We will bring you rain.

(The Raindrops skip around as the Sun stands at the front of the audience.)

FARMER BROWN:
One week, two weeks, three weeks, four! My magic is working more and more.

MRS. BROWN: Look! The magic really is working!

(Children slowly stand up, holding their posters.)

FARMER BROWN:

Thanks to the rain.
Thanks to the sun.
Our spring parade has just begun.
Here come: stringbeans, carrots, tomatoes,
Beets and yellow potatoes.

(Call out the vegetables which the children have drawn. Let them each join the parade.)

ALL: *(March around and sing to the tune of "Three Blind Mice.")*

Spring is here.
Spring is here.
See us grow.
See us grow.
The Farmer is happy for he can see
His garden has good things for you and me.
If you were a vegetable,
What would you be,
Now that spring is here.

WAKE UP!

by Mae Kidman Aldous

Note to the teacher: Simple costumes for this playlet may be made from paper grocery bags. Or draw pictures of the characters on poster boards. Attach lengths of string or yarn to the posters. The actors may wear these hung from around their necks.

Another suggestion is to adapt this playlet for use with stick puppets. Glue brightly-colored, cut-out figures to tongue depressors or ice cream sticks. Use a table covered with brown cloth or paper for the stage. With masking tape, stick on a few cottonballs for snow. Now turn the table on its side, with the table's top facing the audience. The children work with the stick puppets from behind the table, so the audience sees only the figures.

CHARACTERS: Narrator, Tulip, Sun, Caterpillar, Crocus, Moon, Daffodil, Jack Frost.

SETTING: Outdoors. Early spring.

(Crocus, Daffodil, Tulip, and Caterpillar are in place, asleep. If using stick puppets, all characters begin from below the edge of the stage.)

(Enter Sun.)

NARRATOR: Under the ground, Crocus raised her tiny green arms. It felt so good to grow. Earth opened its windows and Crocus stretched up through the ground. She smiled and was happy. She knew it was time.

(Crocus acts out words.)

CROCUS: Wake up, Daffodil.

NARRATOR: Daffodil heard a voice. She started to stir. She started to grow. Up, up, she climbed until she peeked through the white window of snow. *(Daffodil wakes up.)*

DAFFODIL: Hello, Crocus.

CROCUS: Hello, Daffodil. Wake up, Tulip.

NARRATOR: Tulip heard her friend's voice and started to grow. *(Tulip wakes up.)*

TULIP: Hello, Crocus and Daffodil.

NARRATOR: They waved and talked to each other. Then Crocus saw Caterpillar curled up in a ball.

CROCUS: Wake up, Caterpillar. *(Caterpillar doesn't stir.)*

NARRATOR: But Caterpillar didn't want to wake up. She was sleepy. Crocus had to call her again.

CROCUS: Wake up, Caterpillar.

NARRATOR: Caterpillar lifted her head and looked around. *(Caterpillar barely moves.)*

CATERPILLAR: Is it time to wake up?

CROCUS, DAFFODIL, TULIP: Yes! It's wake-up time!

NARRATOR: Caterpillar straightened herself out. *(Caterpillar does so.)*

CATERPILLAR: I'm hungry.

NARRATOR: So Caterpillar started to look for something to eat. *(Caterpillar slowly crawls among flowers.)* Crocus, Daffodil, and Tulip were so excited. They made plans all afternoon. They would be the first to welcome spring. It started to get cold as nighttime arrived. *(Exit Sun. Enter Moon.)* Caterpillar knew her friends needed to be warned. She called to them.

CATERPILLAR: Jack Frost is coming.

NARRATOR: The little flowers quickly tucked themselves in tightly. *(Flowers settle for the night.)* Crocus tried as hard as she could to draw her tender leaves around her. It got colder and colder. *(Enter Jack Frost, blowing.)* She felt the icy breath of Jack Frost.

CROCUS: Help, someone, help!

NARRATOR: Caterpillar heard Crocus call and crawled over to her. *(Caterpillar does so.)* She was so c-c-c-cold. Caterpillar wrapped herself around Crocus to help keep her warm. *(Caterpillar does so.)* The next morning, *(Exit Moon. Enter Sun.)* Sun came out with his shiny, warm rays. Crocus slowy opened her eyes. She stretched up and out, opening her beautiful purple curls for all to see. *(Characters act out narration.)* Caterpillar called to Crocus.

CATERPILLAR: Are you all right?

CROCUS: I'm fine.

NARRATOR: Tulip and Daffodil woke up. *(Do so.)* It was a beautiful day. They heard the breezes whisper, "She's coming!" And they shouted.

ALL: WELCOME SPRING!

REFRESHMENTS

If the children will be sitting at a table to eat, let each one make a place mat and napkin holder. *(See pages 50 and 84.)* These could be made before or as part of the festival.

Here is an idea for an edible favor.

SPRING FLOWERS

Materials needed for each favor: one eggshell half, one pop-bottle cap, glue, one gumdrop, tookpicks, scraps of green construction paper, jelly beans.

1. Glue inside of bottle cap to round end of eggshell. Stand cap on its top. Dry.

2. Place gumdrop in center of eggshell half.

3. Make small leaf shapes from the green construction paper. Glue them onto several toothpicks for leaves on flower stems.

4. Stick one jelly bean as a flower on each toothpick.

5. Stick several toothpick flowers into the gumdrop in a bouquet arrangement.

With fruit punch to drink, choose from the following food suggestions.

VEGETABLE DIP

For colorful, good-tasting, and nutritious refreshments, serve raw vegetables such as carrots, celery, cauliflower, cherry tomatoes, broccoli, and cucumbers. Cut these into pieces for eating with the fingers. Provide a sour cream or yogurt dip.

TASTING BASKETS

Fill small ice cream cone cups with grapes, strawberries, and banana slices. When the fruit is gone, the children may eat the "basket"!

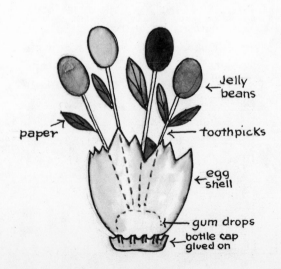

paper
← Jelly beans
← toothpicks
← egg shell
← gum drops
← bottle cap glued on

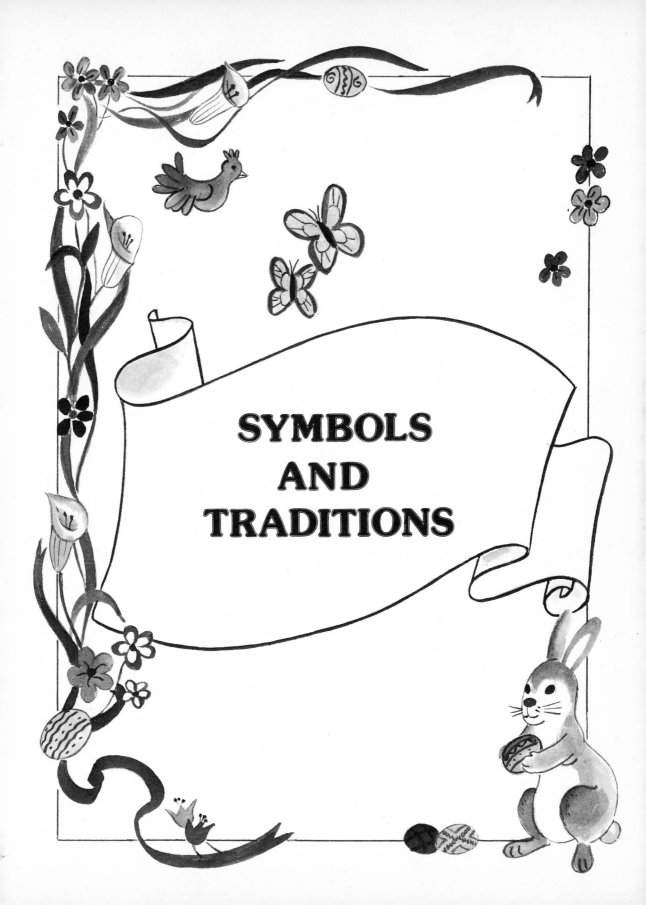

SYMBOLS
AND
TRADITIONS

SYMBOLS AND TRADITIONS

by Ramona Warren

Long before Easter became the most important holiday of the Christian religion, it was a time for a special celebration to welcome the beginning of spring.

Easter is always celebrated the first Sunday after the first full moon in the spring. It is a happy, joyous time. After the long winter, when all nature seems cold and dead, spring suddenly surrounds us with new life that is celebrated with many symbols and traditions that began centuries ago.

EASTER BUNNY

The Easter bunny really started out as the Easter hare in ancient oriental cultures. We don't know when the name was changed or why. We do know that because of their many baby bunnies, it makes sense to use rabbits as symbols of abundant new life.

It was in Germany that the Easter bunny was first connected with Easter eggs in the spring celebration. Children made nests of leaves, moss, or grasses and placed them in their yards or gardens. They believed that during the night the Easter bunny would fill the nests with bright yellow, blue, green, and purple decorated eggs.

In Texas, some people still continue the German custom of burning Easter-eve fires. The children are told that the Easter bunny is burning wild flowers to make his dyes.

ACTIVITIES

1. Sketch a large rabbit shape on a sheet of newsprint. The sketch should show the rabbit's paws in front of his body as if he were holding an egg. (You may use or enlarge the instructions for the Reading Rabbit on page 23.) Have each child make a large construction paper egg, using his favorite color. Let each child take a turn being blindfolded and trying to pin or tape an egg in the bunny's paws. The child whose egg is closest to the bunny's paws is the winner.

2. Devote one session of show-and-tell time to talking about stuffed bunnies brought by the children. Have the children tell how and when they received their bunnies.

3. Sing a song about a bunny. See page 54.

4. Have children write a story about a bunny. Give them story starters such as: a bunny who lost the eggs he was supposed to hide; a bunny who was afraid to go out and hide eggs; etc. Have an aide write down stories dictated by younger children.

EASTER EGGS

The egg is another symbol of new life. Giving eggs at Easter has been an important activity during spring celebrations for centuries.

Children in England, Holland, and France go from house to house asking for Easter eggs. This is similar to the American custom of trick or treating on Halloween.

Eggs that are blessed at church during Easter time in the Orthodox Russian church are part of a special breakfast on Easter day.

German children are given presents that are hidden inside of imitation Easter eggs.

People in many parts of the world dye or decorate Easter eggs. In some countries decorating eggs is considered a great art. Designs are drawn on the egg with beeswax. Then the eggs are dipped in brightly colored dye. The dye colors everything but the design. In Poland, eggs are decorated with crisscross lines, tiny checker-boards, dot patterns, and shapes of plants and animals. No two eggs are alike.

The Easter-egg tree custom came from Germany. To prepare an egg, a tiny hole is pricked at each end of the shell and the inside of the egg is blown out. Then the eggshell is colored, decorated, and hung on a tree or bush.

Some people used to think that Easter eggs had magical powers. They believed that painted eggs buried in the ground at Easter made the grapevines grow well. Some believed that the yolk of an egg laid at Easter time, if kept for a hundred years, would turn into a diamond.

There are many games and contests that use eggs. These include: tossing eggs in the air to see whose goes the highest, using eggs to play a game of marbles, taking turns to try and roll an egg into a hole in the ground, and rolling eggs down a hill. But the most popular Easter-egg activity is the Easter-egg hunt in which children try to find the decorated or candy eggs hidden in their yards or houses.

ACTIVITIES

1. Play a game with Easter eggs. Choose from the two here or on pages 34-37, or 63-65.

Spachen. This game is a duel in which contestants face each other and hold their hard-boiled eggs by the large ends. Contestants stab each other's eggs with the pointed ends. The one who cracks the most eggs wins.

Egg Wink. An egg is placed on the ground. The player takes three steps away from the egg. The player is blindfolded and given a stick. He is allowed to take two steps toward the egg. He then gets three tries to hit and break the egg with the stick. The first person to break the egg is the winner.

Variation: In order to give everyone a turn, have some extra eggs ready to use. Then, everyone who breaks an egg will be a winner.

2. Let the children experiment with blowing out the insides of eggs. Bore a small hole in each end of an egg with a pin, large needle, the point of a nut pick, or a light tap with a hammer and nail. Hold the egg, large side down, over a cup, and blow through the hole until the contents are removed. Then decorate.

3. Bring in books that tell about different ways to decorate eggs. Let the children try some ways other than doing traditional coloring.

4. Make an Easter-egg tree.

EASTER ANIMALS

Baby chicks and lambs are familiar sights at Easter, but did you know that butterflies and peacocks are part of our Easter legends and symbols, too?

The butterfly and peacock are symbols of new life coming from old. The butterfly begins as a caterpillar wrapped in its cocoon. Then from this dead-looking shell emerges a beautiful butterfly.

The peacock sheds its old feathers and, with brilliant new blue and green ones, becomes a renewed bird each spring.

Of course, baby chicks are a symbol of new life. To people long ago, it was startling to see a new and living creature come out of an egg which they considered dead.

The lamb has always had religious meaning and is sometimes used to represent Christ. A long, long time ago, meeting a lamb was considered good luck. In those days there was a superstition that said the devil could become like any animal except a lamb.

ACTIVITIES

1. Let the children make a chick in an egg. See page 48 for instructions.

2. Let the children trace patterns of lambs (see pattern on this page) on sheets of white construction paper folded in half. Have them cut out the lambs and glue on balls of cotton to make them "wooly." The lambs should be able to stand up. You might make a tabletop display or bulletin board by having the lambs stand in imitation grass.

3. Let the children make the Tissue Paper Butterflies on page 19.

4. Have an animals' Easter parade. Let each child choose which animal he wants to be. On a 6" x 9" piece of construction paper, have the child write the name of the animal he has chosen. Attach a string to the name tag and hang it around the child's neck. Then parade around the room or outside, with each child acting out the animal he has chosen to be.

5. Make an animal Easter parade bulletin board (see page 22).

EASTER LILIES AND OTHER FLOWERS

When we think about Easter flowers, the white lily usually comes to mind first. This flower first came from an island near Japan. When it was brought to America, it wasn't even a springtime flower. Since that time flower growers have learned how to make the lily bloom in the spring.

The Easter lily starts out as a hard, brown bulb that has a paper-like shell. The bulb is buried in the earth. The sun shines, the rain falls, and at last a plant grows from the bulb. Soon a beautiful white lily blooms.

All plants and flowers symbolize new life and new hope, but this is especially true of Easter flowers. Some other special Easter flowers include the following.

Narcissus—white or yellow springtime flowers that even grow in the Swiss Alps. They have been part of Easter celebrations for centuries. Maybe you know them by different names, daffodils or jonquils.

Wild Tulips—people in the Middle East decorate their homes at Easter with these flowers. They call them "lilies of the field."

Pussy Willows—these plants are part of spring and Easter festivities in England and Russia was well as in America.

Tropical flowers—these brilliantly colored flowers are taken to church for blessing at Easter by the people of Mexico.

A long, long time ago, people believed trees and plants had magical power and that was why they could turn green in the springtime. Just touching a leaf in the spring was supposed to bring good health and good luck.

Sometimes people would touch one another gently with leafy branches to wish each other good luck. This was called "switching."

ACTIVITIES

1. Visit a local greenhouse/florist, and ask the gardener to show and tell about several plants and flowers. Or, ask the florist or gardener to visit the classroom and give a presentation.

2. Give each child a 6" x 9" sheet of construction paper. Have the child turn it lengthwise and punch a hole about 1/3 down from the top of the paper. Give the child a tissue, and have him pull it by the center through the hole in the paper leaving enough in front to look like flower petals. Have the child tape the tissue down in back. Then have him draw a stem and leaves on the front under the tissue "petals."

3. Make construction paper flowers, and add them to the animal Easter parade bulletin board. (See page 22.)

4. Let the children pretend to be flowers. They may start out by crouching down and pretending to be hard bulbs. Then they slowly stand up as the flowers grow. Finally they fling wide their arms and hands as the blossoms burst forth. This may be done to music. (See page 42.)

5. Make a finger-paint (or pudding-paint) mural of wild flowers and plants. To make colored pudding paint, mix vanilla instant pudding powder with food coloring and enough water so that the paint is easy to spread.

NEW CLOTHES AND THE EASTER PARADE

Whether it's a pair of new shoes or a whole outfit, it's fun to get new clothes.

A long time ago people began wearing new clothes in the spring because they were tired of wearing their heavy winter clothing. The new light clothing represented a new beginning. Some people believed that wearing from one to three pieces of new clothing at Easter would bring good luck all year.

People enjoyed wearing their new clothes so much they wanted to show them to everybody. That's how the Easter parade began.

In some countries it became the custom to take a walk in the country after church on Easter morning. Wearing their new spring clothes, the people would exchange Easter wishes as they walked.

Today, lots of cities and towns in the United States have Easter parades. Some even have judges to award prizes for the prettiest, most elaborate, wildest, etc. costumes. The most famous Easter parade is the one in New York City along Fifth Avenue.

ACTIVITIES

1. Let each child make an Easter hat from a paper plate. First, using a paper punch, make two holes on opposite sides of the rim. The child should cut out the center of the paper plate, tie a length of yarn or ribbon in each hole, and decorate the hat with imitation flowers, ribbon, yarn, etc. Put the hat on, and tie the ribbons under the child's chin.

2. Have the children lie down on big sheets of newsprint. Draw around their bodies. Then let the children use crayons to design new Easter outfits for their "models." Or, you might provide scraps of trims and other items that the children can use to glue on when designing their clothes.

3. Write a poem or a story about an animal who is part of an Easter parade. Younger children may dictate theirs as an aide writes.

4. Plan an Easter parade for a dress-up day close to Easter. Ask the children to wear their best clothes that day. Perhaps they would also like to wear the Easter hats they have made.

EASTER FOODS

Lamb and ham are two kinds of meat often eaten on Easter day. The idea of eating ham on Easter started in England. King William the Conqueror preferred it to the bacon that was normally served. Both come from pigs. In many countries the pig is a symbol of good luck and wealth. In fact, men used to wear little figures of pigs as charms on their watches. Children's piggy banks carry on the idea of associating pigs with wealth and good luck.

Some countries have special kinds of bread and pastry they make for Easter.

In Russia, the bread called *paska* is made with flour, cottage cheese, sugar, raisins, eggs, and milk.

Osterstollen is an oblong loaf of twisted or braided strands of dough made by people in Germany and Austria.

In Ireland, the people eat bread something like our French toast. They call it golden bread.

Mazurka is a pastry from Poland. It is a sweet cake made with honey and filled with nuts and fruit.

Baba is a Polish coffecake. *Baba* is another word for woman. The pan the coffeecake is baked in is shaped like a woman's skirt.

ACTIVITIES

1. Make an Easter cookbook. Ask the children to bring recipes of foods their families make at Easter. Type the recipes on separate pieces of paper, and duplicate enough copies for each child to have a set. Let the children paste or glue the recipes on 6" x 9" sheets of construction paper. Make the sheets into booklets by punching two holes at the left side of each set. Thread a length of yarn through the holes of each book, and tie it in a bow. Have the children decorate the covers of the cookbooks with Easter symbols.

2. Make Easter Bunny Pretzels (see page 51).

3. Make Easter place mats by either weaving strips of construction paper through slits in large sheets of construction paper or by decorating plain white place mats with Easter symbols. Make matching place cards for Easter dinner. Fold a strip of construction paper lenghwise, write a name on it, and decorate with an Easter sticker.

4. Make Bunny Napkin Holders for Easter dinner. (See page 50.)

5. Decorate plain white or colored napkins with Easter symbols. Use them at Easter dinner.

SPRING CLEANING

When people were getting ready for Easter, with new clothes and special food, they wanted their houses to be ready too.

They cleaned their fireplaces, stoves, and furnaces. They washed windows and curtains. They put away heavy blankets and quilts. They brought in fresh flowers to put in the clean rooms. The cleaning was a symbol of a new, fresh beginning. Many families continue the practice of spring cleaning today.

ACTIVITIES

1. Let the children do some special things to "clean" the classroom such as polish chairs and tables, clean the windows, straighten shelves and cabinets, etc.

2. Have children make a spring nature center. Invite them to bring in wild flowers, plants, fruit, etc., and set up a tabletop display. Provide a magnifying glass for children to use to look at the items closely.

3. Make a spring bulletin board (see pages 21-24).

STORIES
TO READ
AND TELL

THE BEST PRIZE

by Beth Holzbauer

Emily pressed her face against the pet store window. "That's the one I want!" she exclaimed. "The duck back in the corner; the yellow fuzzy one. Can't you see him? He's looking right at me. See how bright his eyes are?"

Emily's mother was in a hurry to get home. She answered, "Not now, Emily, not now; we've got to get home."

Emily's smile turned into a frown. For a long time Emily had been wishing for a duck. And just this week Celia Foster had brought one to show the class at school. But every time Emily asked her mother about getting one, the answer had always been the same, "Not now, Emily, now now." Emily took one last glance at the yellow fuzzy duck-

ling and turned to go with her mother.

At home, Father, Brad, and Emily all pitched in and helped Mother. Soon they were sitting down to a good supper.

As they ate, Brad shared exciting news. "There's a big Easter-egg hunt coming up this Saturday at Woodland Park! All children ages five to eleven are invited," Brad said, "and the one who finds the most eggs wins $25.00!"

"The only thing we have to do to enter the egg hunt," Brad continued, "is to decorate a dozen eggs and bring them to the park office by 5:00 p.m. Friday."

"Let's decorate the eggs tonight!" said Emily.

"Not tonight," said Mother. "We don't have two dozen eggs in the house. But I'll buy some tomorrow."

That night, Emily was glad she had something to think about besides the cute little duck she couldn't have.

After school the next day, Brad and Emily quickly changed their clothes. Luckily Mother had bought the Easter-egg dye at the same time she had bought the eggs, so they were ready to begin decorating the eggs. After they colored the eggs in every way imaginable, they set them out to dry.

"What beautiful eggs!" Mother exclaimed when she saw them. "I'll take them to the park office tomorrow morning."

Saturday morning finally came. Both Brad and Emily found baskets to hold their eggs, and then they ran to the car. When they drove into the park, Emily's heart sank. "Look at all these cars! Look at all these people! I'll never win the prize. I'm only six years old. These children are much older and faster!" Emily exclaimed.

"Don't give up yet," Mother said.

"I bet you'll find lots of eggs, and you may even win the best prize."

Over by the big oak tree, there was a man dressed up in a bunny-rabbit suit. The "Big Rabbit" gave the children their instructions and told them the boundaries for the egg hunt. He said that at the "hop" of three (everyone had to hop three times), the hunt would begin.

After the third hop, the children scattered in all directions. In a few minutes Emily lost sight of Brad, and she was on her own. Emily looked in the grass, beside the trees, and under the rocks, but there were no eggs to be found.

Discouraged, Emily thought, "I bet Brad has found twelve eggs by now, and I don't have one!" Everywhere she looked, there where ten children gathered around. "What chance do I have?" she sighed. But then a bright red color in the grass caught her eye. Sure enough, Emily found her first egg. Maybe her luck was changing!

Just then a car slowly went by and stopped. The "Big Rabbit" had told them to be careful of the cars driving through the park. Emily watched the car carefully. Suddenly

a car door opened and a little girl and her father got out. The little girl tenderly carried something yellow in her hands. Tears were running down her cheeks.

Emily's eyes widened as she recognized the girl, Celia Foster, from her school.

"Celia!" said Emily, running to her. "What's the matter?"

"H-Hi, Emily," said Celia, but she was crying too hard to speak.

Mr. Foster put his arms around Celia, wiping her tears with his handkerchief. He spoke to Emily.

"Celia's heartbroken because we're moving away, and we can't take her little duck," he explained. It was then that Emily realized the "something yellow" in Celia's hands was a young duckling. "We thought the park would be a nice place for him. Here, he can be with the other ducks."

"I'm so sorry," said Emily. "I wish I could help. He's such a cute duck. What's his name?"

"B-Beep," replied Celia through her tears. "I w-wish we could t-t-take him with us."

Emily didn't know what to say.

Then Celia said, "Emily, do you want him?"

"Me?" said Emily. "You mean, to keep?"

"Yes," said Celia. "I'd rather give him to you if you want him. At least I'd know he was safe with you."

"I'd love to have him, Celia," said Emily, "and I'd give him the best home in town! But I'll have to ask my mother."

"That sounds like a good idea to me," said Mr. Foster.

"She's right over there by the parking lot," said Emily. "Would you come and talk to her?"

"Of course we will," replied Celia's father.

Emily ran ahead to where her mother waited.

"Mother," she shouted. "Mother, can I keep Celia's duck? Please? Celia has to move and can't take her duck, and they were going to leave him in the park, but it might not be safe, and Celia asked me if I wanted him." The words tumbled out.

Soon the whole story was explained again. "Please, Mom," begged Emily, "can I keep him?"

"How can I refuse?" said Mother. "Yes, Emily, you may keep Beep. I know you'll take good care of him and maybe that will be of some comfort to Celia."

"It will," said Celia. "Guess you'd better take him now."

"Yes," said Mr. Foster. "We really must be on our way."

"Bye, Beep," said Celia, shedding another tear as she gave the duck to Emily. "Bye, Emily. I'm glad that you were here."

"Bye, Celia," said Emily. "Don't worry. I'll take real good care of Beep. Thanks for giving him to me."

"Quack, quack," said Beep. He seemed to know everything would be all right.

As the Fosters made their way back to their car, the whistle blew for the egg hunt to end. Soon Emily and Mother heard Brad's voice.

"Mother! Look what I won!" Brad struggled to carry the large Easter basket he had won. "I won second prize. It's the biggest Easter basket I've ever seen. It's got everything I wanted to buy and more!" Brad pointed to the toy cars, army men, and football that were inside. There was even a baby doll for Emily. And enough candy for the whole family.

"Well, children," said Mother happily, "we've had quite a morning! Brad has won this huge prize and Emily has her duck!"

"The best prize!" said Emily, and she was happiest of all.

TIMOTHY BUNNY AND
THE EGG MYSTERY

by Patricia Stone Martin

Note to the teacher: This story may be read by the teacher to the whole class. The children should number their papers from one to twenty-six. They will fill in the blanks with the correct word: *to, too,* or *two* as the teacher pauses. As an option, with older children, the teacher may let each child take a partner and work in pairs. One will read while the other one writes answers, then reverse. In advance, give these hints: a. to - toward; b. too -also; c. two - number.

Timothy Bunny sniffed. Something smelled good. He hopped quietly over _____ the window and peeked out. There, on the lawn, he saw his _____ sisters and _____ brothers. He could hear them giggling. He heard Amanda say, "Oh, that's _____ funny."

He wanted _____ go out _____, but his mother said he could not. Timothy had been bad the day before. He had gone out in the rain _____ play and had gotten _____ wet and cold. Now he had the sniffles. And it was just before Easter _____. "Easter will not be any fun," moaned Timothy.

"Timothy! What are you doing?" said Mother Bunny. Quickly, Timothy hopped back _____ his bed. "Timothy, you have made your own punishment. You must stay home this Easter. You cannot help us give out the Easter eggs _____ the good girls and boys. Now stay in bed, and if you are good, maybe you _____ will get a surprise."

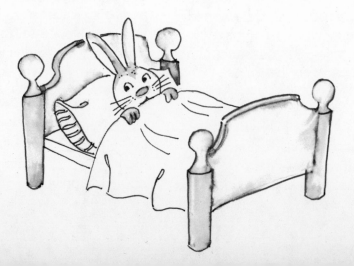

_____ big tears had welled up in Timothy's _____ brown eyes. However, at the mention of a surprise, Timothy brushed them away and snuggled down _____ read a book while he waited. His eyes grew heavier and heavier. Soon he was _____ sleepy _____ keep them open any longer. Timothy began _____ dream....

He opened his eyes and looked around. "Why, this is the new Easter egg factory." Happily he looked down. "I'm sitting on top of a rainbow of eggs." Seeing _____ pretty blue ones below him, he reached down _____ pick them up. Then it happened! All the eggs began _____ move, and Timothy with them. Quick as a wink, he was spinning through space. Faster and faster he turned with ears flapping and paws kicking the air. Down, down, down, he went, and then... BUMP!

Timothy opened his eyes. He was on the floor and his mother and his _____ sisters and his _____ brothers were standing over him laughing.

"Surprise, surprise!" they all laughed, as Mother Bunny handed Timothy a package.

Timothy opened his present. Inside sat _____ pretty blue eggs. "Eggs don't smell like that," he whispered _____ himself. He took a bite. He took another bite. Chocolate! Timothy's cheeks puffed into a smile. "Thank you, Mother, for my _____ yummy surprises," he said happily.

WHAT COLOR IS SPRING?

by Jane Belk Moncure

Note to the teacher: This story will be greatly enhanced by the use of hand puppets and baskets of plastic or hard-boiled, colored eggs. Puppets needed: a yellow duck, a green frog, a pink hippo, a blue bird, and an Easter bunny. If hand puppets are unavailable, flannel board and flannel figures will also work nicely as visuals.

"Spring is yellow," said Little Duck.
"Just look at me.
I'm all dressed up for spring,
you see!"

"Oh, no! Not so!" said Little Frog.
"Spring is green!
Just look at me.
I'm all dressed up for spring,
you see."

"Oh, no! Not so!" said Little Hippo.
"Spring is pink!
Just look at me.
I'm all dressed up for spring,
you see."

"Oh no! Not so," said Little Bird.
"Spring is blue!
It's true!
Just look at me,
I'm all dressed up for spring,
you see."

Then Little Duck, Frog, Hippo and Bird argued very loudly.
"Yellow!" "Green!" "Pink!" "Blue!"
They made such a loud noise . . .
that Easter Bunny came hopping from his Easter-egg workshop!

"Stop!" shouted Easter Bunny!
"What's all the fuss about?"

"The color of spring," shouted Little Frog. "It's green!"
"No! Blue."
"No! Yellow."
"No! Pink."

"No! and yes!" said Easter Bunny. "Why do you argue?
Why do you fight?
When each is wrong,
Yet all are right?

"That's a funny riddle," said Little Duck.

"Come into my workshop!" said Easter Bunny. "I will show you the colors of spring."

Easter Bunny opened the workshop door! The tables were stacked with Easter eggs—hundreds and thousands and even more!

Eggs of yellow, green, pink and blue—orange and red and violet too!

"Spring is many colors!" said Easter Bunny. "I know, because I use the colors of the spring rainbow!"

"That's the answer to the riddle!" said Little Duck. "Spring is many colors! So all of us are right!"
"...Especially when we stand together in a row!"said Little Frog.
"...Like the colors in a spring rainbow!" said Little Hippo.

"Have an Easter egg!" said Bunny. And they did!

THE EASTER STORY

On the first day of the week, very early in the morning, the women took the spices they had prepared and went to the tomb.

There was a violent earthquake, for an angel of the Lord came down from heaven and, going to the tomb, rolled back the stone and sat on it. His appearance was like lightning, and His clothes were white as snow. In their fright the women bowed down with their faces to the ground, but the angel said to them, "Why do you look for the living among the dead? He is not here; he has risen! Remember how he told you, while he was still with you in Galilee: 'The Son of Man must be delivered into the hands of sinful men, be crucified and on the third day be raised again.'" Then they remembered his words.

So the women hurried away from the tomb, afraid yet filled with joy, and ran to tell His disciples. Suddenly Jesus met them. "Greetings," He said. They came to Him, clasped His feet and worshiped Him.

When they came back from the tomb, they told all these things to the Eleven and to all the others. It was Mary Magdalene, Joanna, Mary the mother of James, and the others with them who told this to the apostles. But they did not believe the women, because their words seemed to them like

nonsense. Peter, however, got up and ran to the tomb. Bending over, he saw the strips of linen lying by themselves, and he went away, wondering to himself what had happened.

. . .

While they were still talking about this, Jesus Himself stood among them and said to them, "Peace be with you."

They were startled and frightened, thinking they saw a ghost. He said to them, "Why are you troubled, and why do doubts rise in your minds? Look at my hands and feet. It is I myself! Touch me and see; a ghost does not have flesh and bones, as you see I have."

When He had said this, He showed them His hands and feet. And while they still did not believe it because of joy and amazement, He asked them, "Do you have anything here to eat?" They gave Him a piece of broiled fish, and He took it and ate it in their presence.

He said to them, "This is what I told you while I was still with you: Everything must be fulfilled that is written about me in the Law of Moses, the Prophets and the Psalms."

Then He opened their minds so they could understand the Scriptures. He told them, "This is what is written: The Christ will suffer and rise from the dead on the third day, and repentance and forgiveness of sins will be preached in his name to all nations, beginning at Jerusalem. You are witnesses of these things."

From the Holy Bible (Matthew 28 and Luke 24), New International Version. Copyright © 1973, 1978, 1984, International Bible Society.